The World's Best Fishing Jokes

The World's Best Fishing Jokes

John Gurney

Illustrations by Peter Townsend

An Imprint of HarperCollinsPublishers

AN ANGUS & ROBERTSON BOOK

*First published in the United Kingdom by
Angus & Robertson (UK) in 1987
An imprint of HarperCollins Publishers Ltd
First published in Australia by
Collins/Angus & Robertson Australia in 1987
A division of HarperCollins Publishers
(Australia) Pty Ltd*

Reprinted 1988, 1989 (twice), 1991.

*Angus & Robertson (UK)
77–85 Fulham Palace Road, London W6 8JB
United Kingdom
Collins/Angus & Robertson Publishers Australia
Unit 4, Eden Park, 31 Waterloo Road,
North Ryde, NSW 2113, Australia
William Collins Publishers Ltd
31 View Road, Glenfield, Auckland 10,
New Zealand*

*Text copyright © John Gurney 1987
The author asserts the moral right
to be identified as the author of this work.
Illustrations © Peter Townsend*

*British Library Cataloguing in Publication Data
The world's best fishing jokes
   1. English wit and humour. 2. Fishing – Anecdotes,
   facetiae, satire, etc. I. Gurney, John, 1929–.
   II. Townsend, Peter.
828'.0208*

ISBN 0 207 15622 0

*Printed in Great Britain by
BPCC Hazell Books, Aylesbury*

Introduction

Across the country, indeed all around the world, there is a fraternity of men, women and youngsters whose greatest pleasure in life is to wet a line. They will do it wherever and whenever possible.

They are compelled to prove, perpetually, that they are smarter than the fish. Often they are successful. Too often they are not.

They are a jolly bunch. The jokes that make up this collection are not jokes told against anglers, but stories told by anglers against themselves. It is just as well they have this sense of humour. No-one needs it more than the person at the business end of a fishing line.

All kinds of fishing stories are here—tall tales of bygone catches, sad stories about monsters that escaped, slick dealings with fishing inspectors and, of course, lonely wives who have been deserted for lonely beaches.

We hope that members of this select fraternity will derive some good laughs from reading this, perhaps when it's too rough to go out.

John Gurney

A fisherman who had run out of bait spotted a snake with a frog in its mouth. He trimmed a forked stick and pinned down the snake's head but the snake would not let go of the frog. Then he dropped some whisky on the snake's head. The snake let go the frog to lick up the whisky. The fisherman was able to use the frog for bait. Just as he ran out of bait again he felt a nudge on his leg. The snake was back with another frog in his mouth.

The little old lady asked the fisherman:
    "Doesn't it give you a headache, sitting all day long on the riverbank?"
    "No, madam. Quite the opposite."

A woman walking along a beach came upon a man fast asleep with a fishing rod gripped in his hand. The line was jerking so she woke him up.

"Wake up mister. You've got a bite."

"Oh, would you mind reeling it in for me please?" She did this and landed his fish for him.

"Could you put some fresh bait on the hook and cast it out for me, please?"

She grinned and baited his hook.

"A man as lazy as you should be married and have a son to help him."

"That's an idea. I wonder where I can find a pregnant girl."

A wife said to her husband:

"I don't much like the look of that mackerel you've caught."

"If it's looks you want, why don't you buy a goldfish?"

One of the most unorthodox ways of catching fish was developed by a man who kept bees. He had an old cart horse, the tail of which he plastered with honey. Then he would drive the horse and cart into the river. A cloud of flies was soon attracted by the honey. When the fish jumped out at them, the horse kicked them into the cart.

The parish priest asked young David:
"Which Bible story do you like best, my son?"
"The one about the fellow who just loafs and fishes."

A fisherman trolled his line back and forth in the river. A stranger stopped and asked him:
"Any luck?"
"Not so far."
"Funny. It looks like a really good stream for trout."
"Oh, it is. It really is. They hate like hell to leave it."

L en and Andy invited Des out for a day's fishing in their boat. When they dropped anchor to fish, Des asked:

"Do you boys mind if I fish off the left-hand side of the boat?"

"No. That's okay. We'll fish off the right-hand side."

They did, and all day long they caught nothing. Des, fishing off the other side, kept pulling in one fish after another.

A few weeks later Len and Andy took Des out again. When they dropped the pick, Andy asked Des:

"I suppose you want to fish off the left-hand side of the boat again, eh?"

"No. If it's all right with you boys I'd like to fish off the right-hand side."

And he did. It was like the Sea of Galilee with fish coming from everywhere—on his side. Len and Andy again caught nothing at all. At the end of the day Andy asked Des:

"How the hell do you know which side of the boat the fish are going to be on?"

"Well, when I wake up in the morning I have a look at my wife sleeping alongside me. If she's lying on her left side, I fish off the left side of the boat. If she's lying on her right side, I fish off the right side of the boat."

"That's very interesting. Hang on a minute. What do you do if she's lying flat on her back?"

"Well in that case, obviously, I don't go fishing."

L es and his offsider, Scratch, made a nice thing out of taking tourists out fishing in their boat. One day Les told Scratch about a little problem.

"We've got this party booked for next Wednesday and they're all women. You know we've got no toilet on the boat. How the hell do we explain that to them?"

Scratch wasn't worried at all.

"There's nice ways of saying these things. Like you can use the expression 'evacuate yourself'."

"Well Scratch, how'd it be if you told 'em?"

On the Wednesday morning Les and Scratch were briefing their female charges and Scratch announced:

"There's one other thing, ladies. If you want to evacuate yourselves, you'll have to piss over the side."

T he family were off on holiday. The wife reported: "The car's packed, but now that all your fishing tackle is in, there's no room for the children."

"Have you left enough food for them?"

A fisherman from a railway bridge pulled up a cod nearly two metres long. He threw it across the railway tracks. Not long afterwards a steam train came onto the bridge and the crew stopped to have a yarn with the angler. The cod meanwhile was under the cabin. After a time the train moved off and the fisherman found the wheels had cut off the head and tail of the fish. The cod had shed all his scales in fright, and the heat from the furnace had grilled the fish ready to eat.

"Hey, did I have some luck yesterday," said the fisherman to the stranger as he cast into the middle of the stream.

"Yeah?"

"Yeah! I took thirty-four of the prettiest trout you ever laid eyes on."

"Yeah?" said the stranger. He turned back his lapel to reveal a shiny badge.

"You see that badge? It means I'm an inspector from the Fisheries Department."

The angler thought fast.

"That's nothing. I'm the biggest liar in the country."

Len and Andy were having a beer in the local when a man came in carrying a huge sack. Len told Andy:

"This is the bloke that caught the monster cod. You can ask him about it yourself."

Andy approached the newcomer:

"How big was the cod you reckon you caught, mate?"

"Well, it was too big to fit on my lorry, so I hacked its head off with the axe. I had to bring some evidence to convince the blokes of its size."

"You don't mean to say that big thing in the bag is its head?"

"No way. I couldn't carry the head by myself. This is one of its eyes."

Colin was boasting about the fish he had caught:

"Every fisherman in the country has been after this fish for weeks. Plenty of them hooked him, but he always got away. Then last week I landed him, but I couldn't eat him."

"Why not?"

"He was so full of fish hooks I had to sell him for scrap metal."

David's father asked him:

"How do you get your young brother to dig up so many worms for you?"

"It's easy, Dad. For every ten he digs, I let him eat one."

It was a hot day. The old man fishing from the bank of the stream looked weary and disconsolate. A stranger stopped by and asked:

"Any luck?"

"Mustn't complain."

"Why don't you have a break for a while? Come down to the pub and have a beer with me."

They made their way to the nearby hostelry and the stranger bought the old man a tall, cold beer.

"Tell me something. How many have you caught today really?"

The old man gave a sly grin.

"You're the fifth."

One afternoon the managing director of a big department store was looking through a stack of dockets beside a cash register. He came across one transaction of more than $12 000. Even for a store as large as his it was a really big sale. He asked the department manager:

"Who put this through?"

"A new fellow. Trenery. Only been with us a few weeks."

"Send him up to my office at 9.30 tomorrow morning."

Trenery was duly informed that his presence was required next morning by the managing director. He was a little apprehensive, but presented himself at the appointed time. A secretary showed him in.

"Ah! Trenery, isn't it? Sit down, my boy. Would you like a cup of coffee?"

"No thank you, sir."

"Trenery, my reason for sending for you this morning is that we are planning a new sales training programme, to be used throughout the store. Yesterday I saw from the dockets in your department that you had put through one sale in excess of $12 000. That is a very commendable effort. So much so, that I want you to be a special guest speaker at the sales training programme, so that you can pass on to your workmates the high degree of skill that enabled you to complete what was very likely the biggest transaction ever made in the history of the store."

"Thank you very much, sir, but if you don't mind, I'd rather not. You see, I've only been on staff for a few weeks whereas others have been here many years. If I set myself up as some kind of expert they may easily resent it, and my life in the store could be made miserable."

"I see. Yes. You have a good point there. Perhaps what you can do is describe for me how you made the sale, step by step. I can pass the information along to our trainers, who in turn can give it out at the course without any names being mentioned. Tell me. What was the first item the customer bought?"

"Three dozen trout-fishing hooks."

"I see. What happened then?"

"I sold him half a dozen reels of line, some sinkers, wet and dry flies, and a rod and reel. Next he needed heavy-duty clothing, a hat and a pair of thigh boots. I pointed out that rather than carry his gear backwards and forwards every weekend, he would be much better with a permanent base. I sold him one of our three-room prefabricated cabins. I mentioned that roads into the best spots were fairly rugged and persuaded him to buy a four-wheel-drive vehicle. Then there was the boat and the outboard motor. I think that was all."

"That's amazing. You mean this customer just came in for fish hooks, and you sold him all that?"

"Well, no, sir. He didn't come in for fish hooks at all."

"What did he come in for?"

"He just asked me for directions to maternity wear, so I said to him, 'You look like being in for rather a lame time, sir. Have you tried trout fishing?'"

The ability to tell lies varies with the individual. For example, a short-armed fisherman isn't nearly as big a liar as a long-armed one.

Luigi the fisherman was right down the bay when the sky turned slate grey, a strong wind came up and heavy rain poured down. Luigi's boat sprang a leak and he feared it was going to sink. He got on the radio:

"This isa Luigi. This isa Luigi. The boat isa sinking. The boat isa sinking. Help. Help."

There was no reply. He tried again:

"This isa Luigi. This isa Luigi. The boat isa sinking. The boat isa sinking. Help. Help."

This time his message was picked up by a commercial aircraft and the reply came back:

"Hullo Luigi. Hullo Luigi. This is Captain Williams calling in a Fokker Friendship."

"I don't wanta no Fokker Friendship. I wanta fokker rescue."

A passer-by came upon a man fishing in a pool of rainwater.

"What do you think you might get?"

"Trout."

"What? There are no trout there. In fact there are no fish at all."

"Well, if there are no fish at all, I might as well fish for trout as anything else."

"Anyway, the season's closed for trout."

"Is it? I'm glad you told me. I'll put a bigger hook on and fish for bream."

One fisherman with a reputation for stretching the truth bought a pair of scales. He took them with him whenever he went fishing and insisted on weighing every fish he caught in front of witnesses.

Some months went by and his wife gave birth to a baby boy at home. The doctor borrowed the scales to weigh the child. He weighed fifteen kilos.

An angler was going off for a weekend's fishing. His wife said to him:

"Just in case you don't catch any fish to eat, take along this packet of sausages."

"How do you cook them?"

"It's easy. The same as you do your fish."

The weekend was not a success. The fisherman didn't get a touch. He was bad tempered and hungry when he got home.

"Those sausages you gave me wouldn't feed the cat. By the time I skinned them and gutted them and cleaned them there wasn't enough left to make a decent feed."

In the Scottish lodge there was salmon for breakfast, salmon for lunch and salmon for dinner. One guest couldn't take it any longer and asked for his bill.

"But you've only been here five days."

"With the food I've been getting, I have to hurry up river to spawn."

Bodger was in the fishing tackle department.
"Do you have any left-handed fish hooks please? I'm left-handed."

"We'll go through them and see."

The assistant brought out every box of hooks that he had and examined each one closely. By the time he finished the counter was covered with fish hooks.

"I'm afraid you're out of luck, sir," said the assistant at last. "There don't seem to be any left-handed fish hooks in stock at all."

"Never mind," said Bodger. "Give us a couple of dozen of those. I'll just have to fish off the left-hand side of the boat."

"How long has old Jim Murphy been fishing?"
"I'm not sure, but he's the only member of the angling club with a Louis XIV rod."

Clarence the crab called in to see his friend Squizzy the squid.

"Gee, Squizzy. You look terrible. Are you okay?"

"No, I'm not okay and I feel awful."

"We must do something," said Clarence. "For a start it won't do you any good just lying there on the sea bed. We'll go for a walk. A change of scenery and fresh water will put new life into you."

They set off and before long Clarence spotted a big crayfish up ahead.

"That's my bookie, Fred. Come and I'll introduce you."

When they got closer Clarence hailed the crayfish:

"Good morning, Fred. How are you? How's business?"

They talked for a while, then Clarence said:

"By the way, Fred, here's the sick squid I owe you."

Some of the rivers in the Australian outback have so little water in them that fishermen can tell when a school of fish is approaching by the cloud of dust that it raises.

"I was fishing off the pier here one time when a little minnow about the size of your finger grabbed onto the hook. Next a big cod came and grabbed hold of the minnow. Then, just as I was reeling in the cod, a big shark came and fastened onto it."

"Did you land the shark?"

"No. The bloody minnow let go."

A fisherman had a visitor he hadn't seen for some time. The man noticed that there was now a glass case over the mantelpiece containing a large fish. He asked about it.

"I got it on my last fishing trip. I was on my own in this little rowboat and I fought him for several hours before I got him aboard. Then he thrashed around so much I thought the boat would tip over. I can't swim a stroke and we'd drifted out so far—I had to kill him with my bare hands. It was either me or the fish."

"Well, I must say the fish makes a better decoration."

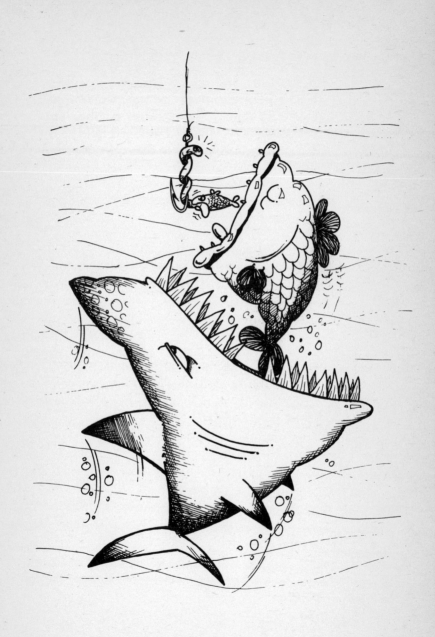

A man had a licence to fish in privately owned waters. A condition was that there was a limit to the number of fish he could take in one day. This was not a problem at first because he caught very little. Then one day the fish began biting so well that he couldn't bring himself to stop when he had reached his limit. He was caught on his way home. His catch was confiscated, and he was taken to court.

The magistrate heard the evidence that he had caught 17 more fish than he was entitled to. He was found guilty and fined $10. The magistrate asked if he had anything to say. He replied:

"Yes, Your Worship. Could I have a photocopy of the court records to show my friends?"

"The wife and I had an awful row. I wanted to go fishing, but she wanted me to visit her mother with her."

"And how is her mother?"

Len was boring his listeners with his story about a snapper he'd once caught.

"Would you believe it took me seven hours to land him, and he went on the scales at 200 lb."

Alf had had enough.

"Did I ever tell you about the time I was fishing over the wreck of an old sailing ship? I pulled up a ship's lantern nearly 200 years old, and would you believe the candle in it was still alight."

"That's ridiculous," protested Len. "Fancy expecting us to believe that."

"Well," replied Alf, "I'll tell you what we'll do. You take 180 lb off your snapper, and I'll blow out my candle."

The old biddie at the market was giving the men on the fish stall a hard time.

"Are you sure these fish are really fresh?"

"Are they fresh? My mate and I have only this minute stopped giving them artificial respiration."

Of all the creatures in the sea, the most intelligent is the dolphin. So intelligent is it, in fact, that within a few days in captivity it can train a man to stand at the edge of its pool and throw it fresh fish three times a day.

A man had spent the whole day fishing off the jetty without anything to show for it. He was sitting with his rod feeling sorry for himself when a woman came along the jetty with her small boy.

"Let me see you catch a fish, mister."

"Don't you do it. Not until he says please."

Two goldfish swam together round their bowl when suddenly one asked the other:

"Do you believe in God?"

"Of course. Who else do you think changes our water every day?"

The day was fine, the sun was warm, but the fish were not biting at all. An angler who had spent the best part of the afternoon getting no result was asked by a local boy:

"How many fish have you caught?"

"None. And I've been here three hours."

"Well, that's not so bad. One fellow fished here for three weeks and didn't catch any more than you've caught in three hours."

A man fishing by himself was a bit put out when a passer-by stopped and watched him. Although he ignored the man he was still there four hours later. At last he said to the fellow:

"Look, if you don't mind, I like to fish alone. Why don't you get yourself a rod and line, find a place, and do some fishing yourself?"

"I wouldn't have the patience."

A friend of ours was complaining about some oysters he'd eaten:

"They're overrated. I had two dozen of them last weekend and only 23 of them worked."

An American spent a lot of money on a two-week fishing holiday in Scotland. He had no luck at all until his last day, when he caught one small salmon. He said sadly to his gillie:

"That one fish has probably cost me around $600."

"Truly? Then perhaps it's as well that you didna catch two."

"It was a really great trip. I got one beauty that was 10 inches."

"That's not much. I've often caught fish that measured 10 inches."

"Between the eyes?"

Two men were preparing to go out for a day's fishing on the bay. While one of them got the boat ready, the other went to his friend's house to pick up some gear that had been left on the verandah. While he was there he saw a man in bed with his friend's wife. Back at the boat he announced that he had some bad news, and said what he had seen. His friend took it calmly:

"Is that all? I was afraid you were going to say the bass weren't biting."

David was missing all afternoon. His mother suspected he had gone fishing but was still worried. He turned up at tea time. She asked him:

"Where have you been all afternoon?"

"Just fishing, Mum."

"If you wanted to go fishing, why didn't you ask me first?"

"Because I wanted to go fishing."

The Parable
of the Fisherman

Behold the fisherman; mighty are his preparations.
He riseth up early in the morning and setteth all his
household in commotion.
He goeth forth full of hope, with companions like unto
himself.
His labours are great; small indeed are his rewards.
Late in the evening he returneth home smelling of strong
drink; the truth is not in him.
What doth it profit a man if he have the patience of Job,
and the wisdom of Solomon,
If in the end the fish are smarter than he is?

"What did Daddy say when his line broke and the
big trout got away?"
"Will I leave out the swear words?"
"Yes please."
"He didn't say anything."

Fred was telling Wally about a great new place he'd found to go fishing.

"Whereabouts is it?" asked Wal.

"You know that old farm just past the edge of town?"

"Yeah."

"Well about five miles further on there's a place with a sign that says 'Private'. You go through the gate—it's got a sign on that says 'Keep Out. Trespassers Prosecuted'. East of that about 200 yards you come to the river and there's another sign, 'Positively No Fishing'."

"What about it?"

"That's the place."

"Fred, you're a lazy devil. Do you think it right to leave your wife to do all the housework while you spend your time fishing?"

"Oh, yes. It's perfectly all right. My wife doesn't need any watching. She works just as hard whether I'm there or not."

After fishing all morning without luck, Fred stopped at the fish shop on his way home.

"Pick me out three big mackerel and throw them over the counter to me will you."

"Throw them? What for?"

"So I can tell my wife I caught them."

The shopkeeper laughed.

"Okay, but it might be better if you take salmon."

"Why?"

"Because your wife came in before and said that if you came in I should persuade you to buy salmon. She rather fancies some for tea."

Two women were talking in the supermarket.

"Ever since Bob took up fishing he's hardly ever at home. He's off on trips every weekend. When I do see him, he seems like a complete stranger."

"How thrilling!"

A trout fisherman came upon two campers with three good-sized trout.

"What do you think of these trout? We got them just by casting a fly into the stream."

"What beauties. What kind of fly did you use? A Royal Coachman, a Silver Doctor, a Red Tag, perhaps, or a March Brown?"

"No, mate. We just cast our tent fly around them."

After a trout-fishing holiday at the lakes, Henry was telling his friends about the sport he had had.

"The fish were so big that the water in the lake went down three inches every time I took one out. By the end of the afternoon I'd caught so many that the boat was high and dry. I had to throw three of them back so it would float."

Terry and Clancy drove off to a fishing resort for a week. They hired a boat the first day and were lucky enough to find a really great place to fish. They decided to mark the place and come back there next day. After they returned the boat, Terry asked Clancy:

"Were you making a mark of that fishing spot of ours, Clancy?"

"To be sure. I put a chalk mark on the side of the boat."

"Clancy! That's no use at all. What if we don't get the same boat?"

The excited angler heaved a mighty heave and reeled wildly until he had a tiny fish three metres up in the air. Its head was jammed against the tip of the rod and it flapped feebly.

"Now what do I do?"

"About the only thing for you to do is climb the pole and cut his bloody throat."

An older man and his young friend had a wonderful day's fishing. As they made their way home the older man said:

"It's been a great day."

"It sure has."

"Will we go again tomorrow?"

"Well, I was going to get married but I think I can put it off."

Young David came home crying his eyes out. His mother asked him:

"What's the matter?"

"Dad and I were fishing and he hooked a really big one. Then, when he was reeling it in, the line snapped and it got away."

"Well, a big boy like you shouldn't be crying about a thing like that. You should have laughed."

David wailed the louder.

"That's what I did."

A man took his family on a holiday down the bay. With them was his wife's mother. Two days after they arrived, the old lady went missing. The wife was very upset but her husband reassured her:

"She's probably staying the night with friends. Don't worry. If she doesn't turn up tomorrow I'll see the police."

But the old lady didn't turn up that night, or the next day either. Accordingly the husband fronted up at the police station. He gave a description of his mother-in-law and the clothes she was wearing. When he had it all down, the sergeant said:

"I'm sorry to have to tell you this, but this morning we found your mother-in-law floating in Deep Creek with twelve crayfish attached to her."

"Gosh. The wife's going to be very upset about this."

"What would you like us to do with her?"

"You have six, and I'll have six, and set her again tonight."

A fisherman on his way home with a good catch was stopped by a nosy parker.

"Been fishing?"

"Yeah."

"You've done well. What bait you using?"

"Chewing tobacco."

"No kidding. How do you use it?"

"You put it on the hook like ordinary bait. You cast like always. The fish snaps at it and pulls back. When he comes to the surface to spit, you bang him over the head with a stick."

There were no further questions.

A generous drunk presented the barman at the pub with a live crayfish.

"Well, thanks very much. I'll take him home for dinner."

"No. He's had dinner. Take him to the pictures."

The local angling club was having its annual dinner and presentation of trophies. When the members arrived they were surprised to see all the chairs spaced out two metres apart. One of them said to the caterer:

"That's a strange way to arrange seats for a party."

"We always do it like that so that members can do full justice to their fish stories."

A farmer was telling a couple of visitors:

"I keep telling my kids not to go fishing in the river. The cod there are so big the little blighters can't hold them. On Tuesday I lost one about three foot six long, and yesterday I lost one more than four feet long."

"My word. It's really bad luck losing fish that size."

"Fish nothing! It's kids I'm losing."

When Digby returned from a camouflaged weekend with his lady friend, his wife asked:

"How was the fishing trip?"

"Very good," replied Digby. "We caught quite a few but gave them to the Guides. By the way, dear, you forgot to pack the flask of brandy and my after-shave."

His wife replied stonily:

"I put them in your tackle box."

A man called at the Riley house. The door was answered by Mrs Riley.

"Good afternoon. I'm looking for Mr Riley."

"I'm Mrs Riley. Can I help you?"

"I'm afraid not. It's Fishing Club business. Could you tell me where I can find him?"

"Just go down to the river and look for a stick with a worm on both ends."

It was ladies' day for the angling club and several of the members took along their wives and daughters. While they were fishing, one of the wives asked the boatman:

"I'm always amazed at the way you fishermen can remember your exact fishing marks. How do you know this spot, for instance?"

"It's perfectly simple. From this side we always get that seagull on the water directly underneath that big white cloud. And on this side we get that little aeroplane directly above the crest of that big wave."

Nearly every night Des used to bring home a few bottles of beer to drink before tea. He discovered that his wife was fed up with this when he went out for a day's fishing. When he unpacked the lunch she had made for him, he found that the sandwiches were particularly tough. He opened them up to find that she had filled them all with bottle tops.

Snowy invited two of his mates home to show them a special surprise. As he brought them in one commented:

"Gosh, your fence is in bad shape, Snowy."

"Yes. The whole house is practically falling to pieces. You know how hard it is to get anything done these days. Building material is so scarce and everything."

"What's this surprise you want to show us?"

"Out here in the back garden. Look at that."

He showed them a spanking new fishing boat.

"Isn't she a beauty? Thirty feet long, nine feet beam, all the latest fittings. I built every bit of her myself."

A fisherman dropped into a local pub carrying a brand new fishing rod. One of the regulars admired it:

"That's a beautiful rod you've got, mate."

"Yes. It is a good one. I got it for the wife."

"Wish I had half your luck. I'd like to work a swap like that."

The women at the bridge party were all admiring a huge stuffed shark mounted over the mantelpiece. Their hostess smiled proudly:

"My husband and I caught that on a deep-sea fishing trip."

"What's its stuffed with?"

"My husband."

It was cold and wet and windy. Two men met in the street.

"Where're you going?"

"Football."

"You're mad. In weather like this? Why don't you come with me?"

"Where are you off to?"

"Fishing."

Young Jimmy used to boost his pocket-money by going fishing and selling his catch to the people in the village. One Sunday he had sold all his fish except for one. The only house he hadn't tried was way up the top of a cliff. He toiled his way up the steep path but when he finally knocked, the door was flung open and a man shouted rudely:

"No fish."

Jimmy made his way back down the cliff path. Just as he reached the bottom he heard a voice calling to him from the house he'd just left. There was a woman at the door, waving to him. Wearily he dragged himself all the way back up the steep path. When he reached the house the woman snapped:

"And we won't want any fish next Sunday either."

If you ever catch a whale do you know where to get it weighed?

At a whale-weigh station.

The locals warned the city slicker:
"Don't put a net into this river. The inspector here, named Riley, hates nets. He'll blow off your head with his shotgun if he catches you at it."

The townie thought he knew better. Early next morning he began pulling in his net when a voice behind him boomed:

"Drop that net, put your hands up and don't move or I'll blow off your head."

The city man did as he was bid and asked:

"And who might you be?"

"I'm Riley, the fisheries inspector."

"Well that's a relief," said the city slicker. "I was afraid you might be the owner of the net."

A pelican said to his mate:
"That's a good sort of fish you've caught there."
"Yes. It fills the bill nicely."

Wally asked a couple of his drinking mates:
"Come down to my shack on the bay next weekend. The place is teeming with fish. It'll be good relaxation for you both."

"Thanks, Wally. We'll do that."

On Friday evening they presented themselves at Wally's place all ready to go. One of them asked the host:

"What's all that gear in your trailer?"

"It's only the material for a few odd jobs I'd like you lads to help me with down at the shack. I want to rebuild the old fireplace, put up some fresh spouting, make a couple of gates, and put a few new ribs in the boat. After that we can really give the fish a hiding."

"Why do you always take your wife with you when you go fishing?"

"It's easier than kissing her goodbye."

The stall at the market had a great wire basket full of live lobsters crawling slowly around. A little old lady studied them for some time and then asked the stall holder:

"Are these lobsters fresh?"

"Are they fresh? Madam, do you think I wind them up every morning?"

After the wedding the young couple drove off on their honeymoon. Just past the river they stopped and the groom went off through the trees. After an hour his bride went looking for him. He was fishing.

"What's going on?" she demanded.

"Are you nagging already?"

"How did the fishing trip go?"

"Really well. The empties alone brought £185."

The fisherman was showing his friend the photographs taken on his fishing holiday.

"You got some beauties."

"I know, but my daughter did even better. She caught a twenty-four-year-old doctor."

Out in a fishing boat one of the men asked:
"Would you know how to tell your position if you were out here in a thick fog, with no compass, no sun, and a slack tide?"

"No. How?"

"You cut three feet off your best fishing line and tie your watch on the end. Then you swing it round your head three times and let 'er go."

"How does that tell your position?"

"Because your watch would go west."

There were fishermen all along the river bank fishing without success. One of them asked a local:

"Don't they ever catch fish in this river?"

"Don't know. I've only been watching for three years."

Two anglers in a boat were not having much luck. One said:

"Thompson's boat's been anchored in the same spot for hours. Put the binoculars on them and see whether they're catching anything."

His mate studied the other craft for a moment, then said:

"What a nerve he's got."

"What's wrong?"

"Thompson's sitting on the deck watching us through his telescope to see what we're catching—the nosy old coot."

An angler was telling his friend:
"I had a funny dream last night. I dreamed I was going up to Heaven on a ladder. The bottom of the ladder was right in our angling club. The members who were climbing up had to put chalk marks on the side of the ladder for all the tall stories they'd told about the fish they'd caught. I looked up and saw another member coming down in a tearing hurry."

"Who was it?"

"It was you. You said you were coming down for more chalk."

Two fishermen were talking.
"I love fishing. The fresh air. The solitude. Man against nature. Matching wits with the denizens of the deep. The thrill of playing and landing your cunning adversary. Tell me. Why do you fish?"

"My son's learning the bass guitar."

The Billy Graham crusade was in Northern Ireland. Late one afternoon Dr Graham was walking along the cliffs when he came upon two Protestant lads pulling a Catholic up the cliff out of the water by a rope. He spoke to them:

"This is a fine act of Christian charity that you're doing. You can be sure that the good Lord will bless you both for it."

As he walked away one of the lads asked the other: "Who was that?"

"That was Dr Billy Graham. He knows more about the Bible than any other man in the world."

"Perhaps he does, but he doesn't know much about shark fishing."

"Your father's an expert on fishing, is he?"

"That's right. The day before he goes he can tell you exactly where the fish will be biting. And the day after he can tell you exactly why they weren't."

Les was looking very depressed at the angling club, so his mate asked him:

"What's up with you today?"

"It's the wife. She's just delivered an ultimatum. Either I give up going on fishing trips all the time, or she's going to clear out and go back to live with her family. Gosh, I'm going to miss her."

A husband and wife were surf fishing together. The husband hooked a big salmon, but as he reeled it in it became tangled in a large clump of seaweed. He yelled to his wife:

"Quick! Race in and free the line before the sharks get to him."

The teacher asked David:

"Do fish grow fast?"

"I'll say they do. My Dad caught one last week and it gets bigger every time he talks about it."

Ted and Bruce were out fishing in a boat when Ted had the first touch of the day. As he set the hook he said:

"Wow! I've hooked a big pike or a carp."

After he played it for a couple of minutes he told Bruce:

"Maybe it's a small bream the way it's darting around. No, I think it might be a dace."

But when he landed it:

"A miserable stickleback!"

It was the only bite they had, and after an hour or so they headed back to the jetty. One of their friends asked them:

"Did you have any luck?"

Bruce laughed and held up their single fish:

"Ted caught five different kinds of fish—pike, carp, bream, dace and stickleback. This is it."

"Did you have any trouble explaining the fishing trip to your wife?"

"I sure did. She found out I didn't go."

A fisherman stood at the water's edge on a lonely beach. There was not another soul in sight. Just the headland at each end of the beach, and the cliff rising tall behind him. The sun sparkled on the water and he felt completely in tune with Nature.

Suddenly, from around the headland to his right, came a young woman, running on tiptoe along the surface of the water. She was completely nude. She ran into the little bay, across the beach, and straight up the sheer face of the cliff.

After she was lost to view, the fisherman began to wonder whether he had imagined the whole thing. Then, around the same headland, there came a luxury launch. It made its way slowly in to the beach. The skipper hailed him:

"Did you see a girl come past here, running along the top of the water?"

"Yes, I did. She headed up the cliff and disappeared. What's the story?"

"She's the secretary of one of my suppliers. I asked her if she might like to spend a day on my boat and she was quite agreeable. I laid on a rather special lunch with champagne and all the trimmings, and afterwards suggested that we go below together. Again she was quite agreeable. I put the boat on automatic and we stripped off to go to bed. When she was naked she was the most delightful sight I'd ever seen. Of course, you know about that yourself.

"But once we got into a clinch, she was the tightest, softest . . . And then of course the engine conked out. It's just behind the head of the bunk so I reached over to get it going again. As it fired I must've touched the spark plug . . ."

"I dropped a watch in the River Thames a year ago and I just fished it up. Would you believe it's still running."

"The same watch?"

"No. The River Thames."

Two men fishing off the rocks were approached by a stranger.

"Excuse me, fellers. Can you spare me a bit of the bait you aren't catching any fish on?"

"We aren't getting them on shrimp or mussel. You're welcome to try some of that."

"I'd like to try not getting them on pilchards or sand worms if you've got any."

"Sorry. We can't help you."

"Oh well. I might as well go home as stick around without the wrong kind of bait to be not catching them on. See you."

The waiter in a country pub brought a guest his dinner.

"You'll enjoy this fog fish, sir. I caught it myself."

"Fog fish? I've never heard of them before. How do you catch them?"

"Well, when there's a very thick fog on the coast, we drop a few charges of gelignite into the water. The fish get blown up into the fog. Because they're still groggy they start swimming around in it. That's where I come in.

"I just lean a ladder against the fog and hack big holes in it with a carving knife. The fish don't expect the holes, so they fall out into my hands. You wouldn't read about it."

The priest of the parish challenged one of his flock: "Terrence. I hear that the reason you didn't come along to church yesterday was because you were playing golf."

"That's not true, Father, and I've got the fish to prove it."

The launch was moored in the middle of a fierce storm. One of the fishermen on board asked the skipper:

"I've never seen it blow so hard. What are we going to do?"

"It looks as if we'll have to try the crowbar trick."

"The crowbar trick? What's that?"

"We'll poke a crowbar out the porthole. If it only bends in the wind, we can go fishing. But if it snaps off, we'll turn in and have a sleep."

Two fishermen away on a trip met an old timer who told them:

"I used to travel thousands of kilometres every year to fish for marlin, trout, salmon, you name it. But these days I'm just as happy tossing a line into that horse trough over there."

"You wouldn't get any fish doing that."

"No, but by golly it's convenient."

Back from holiday a fisherman was telling his neighbour about a big pike he caught while he was away.

"Thirteen pounds it was, and took me more than two hours to land."

His little daughter chimed in:

"Yes, and Daddy was so good. He gave it to my little pussy to eat."

A clergyman with his two beautiful daughters was walking along the river bank. They came upon an angler and, after exchanging pleasantries, the clergyman said:

"I too am a fisherman, but I fish for men."

The angler eyed the girls appreciatively:

"I imagine you catch quite a few, judging by the bait you're using."

A fisherman was intrigued to see a small boy baiting his hook with a dead mouse.
"What are you fishing for?"
"Catfish."

Jimmy promised before he went away that he would send home the first trout he caught. Five days after he left, a parcel arrived. His wife looked at it and said to the messenger:
"He never does anything right. I asked for a trout and this is marked COD."

At the end of the day Fred was contemplating his empty basket when a passer-by asked:
"What are you fishing for?"
Fred replied:
"I keep asking myself the same question."

Les's launch was stuck on a sandbar and he couldn't make it to his moorings. He called out to a couple of his mates in a dinghy:

"Can you stop at my place and tell the missus I won't be home until the tide comes in? I'm stuck on the sandbar."

"Okay."

On the way home they stopped at Les's place and told his wife:

"Les won't be home for some hours. He's stuck over the bar."

"That's nothing unusual," she replied. "Which pub is he at this time?"

A young girl took some lunch to her father fishing on the river bank.

"Have you caught any, Dad?"

"Well, if I catch this one that I'm after now, plus two more, I'll have three."

On the river bank the fisheries inspector was going through one man's bag.

"You've got five perch. That's okay. I have to make sure you've got no trout."

"I'm only fishing for perch, inspector. I haven't even got a trout licence."

"Hang on. What's the idea of having that big trout tethered there?"

"He kept taking the bait and spoiling my perch fishing. I got sick of him in the end and tied him up until I go home. Then I'll let him go."

"What it is to be popular! The missus lined up a barbecue at our place today. I forgot all about it and went fishing."

"Did you catch anything?"

"I did when I got home."

Two really keen fishermen set out into the bay in a pea soup fog.

"We must be mad going out fishing in this."

"We'll be okay. Take this compass and steer south-west for half an hour. Then we'll drop anchor and try our luck."

But after they'd been going for a while the man at the rudder said:

"Gosh! The watch has stopped. We must have gone more than half an hour. Get the anchor ready."

Shrouded in grey mist, they had some of the best fishing they could remember. Eventually they upped anchor and headed north-east back to the angling club. When they brought their catch in the members crowded round.

"What a great box of fish! Where did you get them?"

"That's the trouble. We don't know where we were."

Professional fishermen are unable to answer the question:

Does fishing result in net profits?

An angler was having a great afternoon fishing a river. He had a creel full of beautiful good size fish. A farmer came pushing a barrow along the bank. The fisherman said to him:

"Gee, this is certainly a great spot for fishing. I've caught some beauties."

The farmer was dubious.

"I wouldn't eat those fish if I were you. Thousands of myxomatosis rabbits have fallen into that stream and been eaten by the fish. Horrible stories have been told about how the poison affects the fish."

"Is that so? I'm glad you told me. There's no use in taking this lot home. I'll give you a quid if you'll bury them for me somewhere."

"Yeah. I'll help you out."

When the angler had packed up and gone, the farmer took the fish home to show his wife.

"Guess what we're having for tea tonight. A feed of fresh fish."

A young woman was admiring a young man sitting on the river bank. Her father asked her:

"You're not interested in him, are you? He's a very poor fisherman."

"Maybe so, but he's also a very rich stockbroker."

Two American Indians were fishing from a canoe when one pulled in a beautiful mermaid. He freed her from the hook and threw her back.

"Why?" asked his friend.

"Not why. How?"

A visitor was asking an old timer about his hunting. "I haven't been hunting at all lately. In fact the last duck I shot was a rabbit. When I took it over to the pub they said it was the nicest fish they ever tasted. No kidding, it must've weighed six pounds if it was an inch."

An old timer walked into the bar of a coastal pub carrying a wet sack that dripped water all over the floor of the bar. The publican asked:

"What you got in the sack?"

"It's me pet octopus."

"Give us a look."

The old timer reached down into the sack, pulled out the octopus and plonked him on the bar. Arms and legs waved everywhere.

"Very interesting," said the publican, "but I'm not sure I want one of them things in my bar."

"It's okay," said the old timer. "He's tame. And not only that, but he's trained. Do you know that this octopus can play any musical instrument that you give him. Look at this."

He gave the octopus a flute and it played a little tune. He took it away and gave him a violin and the octopus played again. After several other instruments had been demonstrated the publican said:

"Any musical instrument, eh? Any musical instrument at all?"

"That's right."

"Stay here for a few minutes will you?"

The publican went away and after a time came back with a set of bagpipes.

"Can he play this?"

"Course he can. Just give it to him."

The publican gave the bagpipes to the octopus. The octopus crawled round one side. Then he came back and crawled round the other side. Then he crawled over the top. Then he dived underneath.

"Why isn't he playing them?" asked the publican.

"He will. He will. Just as soon as he discovers he can't screw 'em."

"Just how big was that monster bream that got away from you, Denny?"

"Well, I had 50 yards of new line on my reel. I dropped the line over the side and the bream grabbed the bait and took off upstream. The last of the line ran off the reel just as the bream's tail passed the boat."

A fisherman in north Queensland caught an enormous groper. He started to clean it, but dropped his knife down the monster's throat. He crawled in after it and was feeling around when a man came up beside him on horseback.

"Whatcha doin' there?"

"Tryin' to find me knife."

"You've got no hope, mate. I've been in here a week tryin' to find a herd of sheep."

The party fishing out in the bay struck a patch of rough weather. One of the men was so sick he lost his false teeth over the side. Later on as they were cleaning their catch in a sheltered inlet, another member of the party, for a joke, took out his own false teeth and pretended to find them in a big bass he was cleaning. He passed them to the first man. He studied them closely and threw them over the side.

"Not mine. Some other poor coot must've lost them."

The inspector confronted two men camped by a river.
"Who owns that line set in the river down there?"
"I do."
"Don't you know that fishing is prohibited in this area?"
"Well if you must know, I'm not fishing. I just tied a bottle of beer to the end of a line and left it in the river to cool."
"Is that so? In all my experience, it's the first time I've ever seen a bottle of beer swimming around in circles and coming up every few minutes for air."

An odd-looking character turned up at the angling club. One of the members asked his friend who he was.

"He's a visiting piscatorial authority. He's collecting angling records."

"Is he being well received?"

"He certainly is. Every angling club in the country is receiving him with open arms."

A trout fisherman was at it for two weeks before he landed his first fish. He sent off a telegram to his wife:

"I've got one. It's a beauty. Weighs eight pounds. Be home Saturday."

The next day a telegram was delivered to his hotel from his wife:

"I've got one. It's a beauty. Weighs seven pounds. Looks like you. Come home at once."

A Fisherman's Prayer:

God grant that I may catch a fish
So big that even I
When speaking of it to my friends
May never need to lie.

David's mother cautioned him:
  "I know you've got waders on, but don't go right into the middle of the river when you're fishing. The current is strong and you might get swept away."
  "But, Mum, Dad always goes into the middle of the river."
  "Yes, but that's all right. He's insured."

A man was sitting with a fishing line dangling into the fountain of the city square. A passer-by enquired:
  "Have you caught anything?"
  The sportsman replied:
  "You're the fourteenth."

An inspector from the Australian Fisheries Department boarded a launch that had just come in.

"I want to inspect your catch."

"We only got the one fish—this fifteen pound snapper. It was a funny thing. When we opened the snapper we found it had swallowed this two pound pike. But that isn't all. Inside the pike was this whiting."

The inspector was not impressed.

"Sorry, but I'll want your name and address. That whiting is undersize."

Fred asked his wife:

"Why does a woman say she's been shopping when she doesn't buy anything?"

His wife shrugged, and said:

"Why does a man say he's been fishing when he hasn't caught anything?"

The manager of the Riverside Caravan Park always greeted the fishermen at the end of the day by asking: "How did you do?"

Late one afternoon he saw a man's head appear and asked his usual question:

"How did you do?"

The response was quite angry. Then he saw that the man was carrying a rug and cushion, and had a pretty girl by his side. He wasn't even carrying a hand line.

Two fishermen were given the use of a fishing shack by a friend. As they arrived, one said:

"Fred said he'd leave the key and a note under the dish on the stool outside. Here it is, just like he said."

"And the note telling us where to find everything. What's it say?"

"The tea is in a cartridge box over the fireplace, the sugar is in a jar labelled 'Horse Liniment' and the biscuits are in a tin marked 'Rat Poison'."

A man wanted a piano tuner and was given an address. When he went looking for it he couldn't find it so he went into a fish shop to ask for directions. The little Greek behind the counter couldn't be more helpful.

"You coma to da right place. A poun' a tuna coming up."

One moonlit night the rector, the vicar and the Catholic priest were fishing from a small boat. Presently the rector stood up.

"Excuse me, gentlemen. I have to answer a call of nature."

Stepping out the right side of the boat, he walked across the water to the bank six metres away. After a time he returned the same way.

Then the vicar also said that he would answer a call of nature. He stepped out the right side of the boat, walked across the water to the bank, and returned in the same way a few minutes later.

This was too much for the Catholic priest, who decided that he couldn't be left out. He stepped out the left side of the boat and at once sank out of sight. The vicar said ruefully to the rector:

"We mustn't have told him about that sandbank."

Two fishermen had been at it all day. In the late afternoon one said:

"We've been here since early morning and haven't had a touch."

"Don't be impatient. They'll come on soon."

They were still there in the early hours of the morning.

"Gosh, it's almost daylight and we still haven't had a bite."

"They'll come on presently."

The sun was high when the first man announced:

"I've had enough of this. It's eleven o'clock. I'm going home."

"Gee, you're easily discouraged, aren't you?"

Father Cassidy was a keen fisherman and was a bit put out at having to do a wedding when he could have been down at the river. He asked the bride:

"Do you promise to love, honour and obey this man?"

"I do."

"Okay. Reel him in."

A woman said to the proprietor of her fish shop: "You've got a good business here. You're making a lot of money. How is it that you're so smart?"

"Because of the special fish I eat."

"You'd better sell me some."

"Sure." He sold her the fish.

Later she came back.

"That special fish you sold me at such a price. When I ate it I discovered it was only herring."

"See? It's working already."

A fisherman accidentally left his catch under his seat on the bus. The next issue of the local paper had this advertisement:

"If the person who left a parcel of fish on the No. 47 bus would care to come down to the depot, he can have the bus."

The town loafer approached a farmer friend.

"Have a look at this trout I just caught. You can have it for the price of two pints, and I'll clean it for you for another fifty pence."

"Okay. You can clean it, but I want you to leave the eyes in."

"Leave the eyes in? What for?"

"So it'll see me through the weekend."

A man went into a sporting goods shop.

"You know all that expensive fishing tackle you sold me when I was in here last time?"

"Yes, sir."

"You know you told me it was well worth all the extra money because of all the fish I was going to catch with it?"

"Yes."

"Well would you mind telling me again? I'm getting discouraged."

A fisherman on holiday in the country got up very early and headed for the river. In the main street he heard a clock strike four and thought to himself:

"So much for these country people being early risers. The place is deserted."

Then he saw a farm-hand and called out:

"Fine morning."

"Yes, but it wasn't half cold first thing."

Tom and Herb were fishing after dark from the jetty on the edge of the lake.

"Gosh, Tom, these mosquitoes are bad, aren't they?"

"They're not giving me any trouble."

"I don't know about you, but every time one bites me he passes out straws to all his mates."

Two Irishmen travelled to Scotland looking for work but had no luck. They were hungry and short of cash. Walking around they saw two Scots on a bridge. One was holding the other over the side by the ankles. When they asked what this might be, it was explained to them that the two men were tickling trout. Sure enough, a few minutes later the man below pulled out a good-sized fish.

"Let's find a bridge of our own, Terrence, and we'll try our luck."

Presently they found a bridge and Patrick held Terrence over the side by the ankles. He was there 20 minutes and having no luck when suddenly he called to Patrick:

"Pull me up, Pat. Quick."

"Have you got a beauty, Terrence?"

"No, I haven't, but there's a great train coming."

"The wife's run off with my best friend."

"That's no good."

"Now I'll have to go fishing without him."

All along the pier there were fishermen hauling in fish. Among them was a young schoolboy fishing with a bent pin and a ball of string. Beside him was a fish weighing over 10 kilos. His mate came down to the pier and asked him about his catch:

"What kind of fish is it, Mike?"

"I don't know, but that fellow over there told me it was a bloody fluke."

Conversation heard in the bar of an Australian coastal pub:

"Now let's get this straight. You've got an uncle up north named Sunday, and he's got a fishing boat named Wednesday."

"That's right. What I said was that Sunday caught a barramundi on a Tuesday from the Wednesday."

"Whereabouts was this?"

"Thursday Island."

There was a crowd of more than five thousand bearded characters in long robes standing on the bank of the Sea of Galilee. They had been there for hours and it was lunch time. The only food that came to light was five barley loaves and three fishes.

Philip said to James:

"Look at that. Another typical logistics cock-up."

The lady of the house was complaining to her fisherman husband:

"Why is it that you never take me out to dinner the way you used to before we got married?"

"There'd be no point. You don't go on feeding bait to a fish after you've caught it."

Alex was back from a trout-fishing holiday. Tom was asking him about it.

"Did you fish with flies?"

"Fish with them? I fished with them, camped with them, ate with them, and even slept with them."

Little Cathy asked her mother:
"Mummy, do all fairy stories start with 'Once upon a time'?"

"No dear. Sometimes they start with 'Thisa fish must've been at least three feet long'."

A boy's parents gave him the job of minding his four-year-old sister while they went shopping. He decided to take her fishing with him. He told his parents later:

"I'll never take her again. I didn't catch a thing."

"Why didn't you explain to her that you didn't want any noise? She'd have been quiet."

"That wasn't the trouble. She ate all the bait."

Harry was introduced to a big-game fisherman who held several records.

"What was the biggest fish you ever caught, Les?"

"Dunno. We couldn't get him on the scales. But I'll tell you what. A snapshot we took of him weighed six pounds."

A man was fishing for trout beside a golf links. He hooked a beauty and was so excited that he tossed the fish over his head. It came off the hook and flew onto the golf course. While he was looking for it a golfer asked him what he was doing. The fisherman replied:

"Looking for trout. They often leave the water and wriggle around the grass looking for grasshoppers."

As he spoke, he picked up his missing trout. For the rest of the day there were golfers up and down the river bank looking for trout.

Two women were talking after their aerobics class.

"I thought I saw your husband fishing down at the river."

"Had he caught anything?"

"A couple."

"It couldn't have been my husband."

Ted and Bruce stopped at Henry's place.

"Bruce and I are going out on the bay fishing. Do you want to be in it?"

"Fishing? Gosh, anyone who goes out fishing on a day like this ought to be certified. It will probably blow like the devil and a man will be as sick as a dog, get no fish, and get soaked to the skin into the bargain. Probably finish up with pneumonia or something."

"Well if you feel like that about it we'll be getting along. See you."

"Hang on. What's the idea? Are you two trying to sneak off without me?"

An angler felt guilty about fishing on Sunday. He said to his companion:

"Maybe we shouldn't really be here. Perhaps we should have gone to church."

"Well I certainly couldn't have gone. My wife's sick in bed."

Alf went to visit Herb and found him fishing in the cellar.

"What's this then?"

"I got sick and tired of pumping it out so now I've had it stocked."

Snowy was describing the pike he'd caught the week before. His friend asked:

"How big was it?"

"Biggest I ever saw," said Snowy.

"Doesn't tell me much. Measure with your hands."

Snowy looked around the room.

"Okay, but we'll have to go outside."

"How did the trip go?"
       "Not much good. We caught only one fish."

"What did you do with it?"

"It was so small we got a couple of other blokes to help us throw it back."